Famous Dogs

(& a Cat)

Changing History
One Dog
(& Cat)
at a Time

By

Pat McGrath Avery

&

Luke the Detective Dog

ISBN: 978-1-937958-34-3 (Trade Paperback)

ISBN: 978-1-937958-35-0 (eBook)

ISBN: 978-1-937958-36-7 (iBook)

Red Engine Press

Bridgeville, PA

Printed in the United States.

Dedicated to dog lovers everywhere

TABLE OF CONTENTS

LUKE THE DETECTIVE DOG

Hi, my name is Luke. I'm a Bichon and I live with Mom, Dad and my sister Peanut, a Teacup Poodle.

I wear many different hats. My most important job is making Mom and Dad happy and warming their hearts. I try to make them laugh throughout the day.

They give me kindness, love, and lots of treats. That's every dog's dream.

I also help my mom write mysteries. In them, I am Luke the Detective Dog and I help Hap Lynch, the other hero, solve crimes. I stay close to Mom when she's working on her computer because she needs me to give her ideas and to keep her motivated.

We write dog books together. In them, I'm Luke the Reporter Dog and I interview other dogs — and sometimes cats. I love to find out what other animals think. I've discovered that most of us are happy, content, and that we do our best to take care of our families.

If a dog has a forever home with someone who loves him, he's a happy camper. Pretty simple when you think about it. I think that's what people want too.

Mom also helps people write their own stories. When she tells me about them, I always am curious about where dogs fit in. I decided to research some famous — and not so famous — dogs that have played a part in the history of dogdom.

I found out that dogs have always helped people. Sometimes, they have had an important part in changing history. Two of my favorite heroes from my research are Balto and Seaman. Balto helped save a town and Seaman helped explore a country

I looked a long time to find a famous Bichon and I did. You'll read about Dakota — he's a handsome fella. I hope you enjoy reading the stories about all the dogs — and a cat.

CHAPTER 1

SEAMAN, EXPLORER, THE LEWIS AND CLARK EXPEDITION

Seaman was born in Pittsburgh, Pennsylvania, and became a famous dog explorer. He helped U.S. Army Captain Meriwether Lewis and his friend, William Clark. Seaman and Lewis adopted each other in 1803.

He was a Newfoundland, a breed of giant, hard-working dogs that excel at water rescue and fishing. They are known to be strong, calm, and loyal. They are natural swimmers and have a thick double coat and webbed feet.

When Lewis and Clark explored the United States territory a long time ago (in 1804), they depended on Seaman to keep danger away. Captain Lewis kept a journal and wrote about some of Seaman's adventures.

The expedition, known as Lewis and Clark's Corps of Discovery, left from Washington, DC. They traveled in canoes down the Ohio and Mississippi Rivers to St. Louis. From there, they paddled up the Missouri River across the Rocky Mountains to the Columbia River and the Pacific Ocean. The entire trip, there and back, took four years.

They crossed through nineteen states for more than 4,600 miles. The states included Delaware, Maryland, Virginia, Pennsylvania, Ohio, West Virginia, Kentucky, Indiana, Illinois, Missouri, Kansas, Nebraska, Iowa, South Dakota, North Dakota, Montana, Idaho, Washington, and Oregon.

Seaman's main job was to protect Lewis and the other members of the expedition. He guarded them the entire trip. Lewis wrote about several occasions when Seaman saved them. Everyone depended on him and he became "our dog" rather than "Lewis' dog."

Seaman loved roaming and exploring the prairies with Lewis. They spent hours tromping through the prairie grass. He loved the wind in his face as they paddled the canoes. In fact, to Seaman the entire expedition was a great adventure. Each day brought new smells, sights, and sounds.

Seaman smelled his first buffalo herd before he heard it or saw it. He loved Sacagawea, the Shoshone Indian woman who joined the expedition and acted as interpreter to the Indians they met along the way. It is easy to imagine him as her baby son's protector.

Wild animals threatened the early explorers. Seaman stayed alert day and night to the smell and sound of animals that could hurt his people. When he started barking, everyone looked for danger. Although buffalo and bear outweighed him, Seaman had the heart of a warrior. His weapons included a ferocious bark, an ability to run fast, and a protective spirit.

One evening as Lewis walked along the shore, a buffalo calf followed at his heels. Seaman stayed close to Lewis and kept the calf at a safe distance.

Another evening, a large buffalo bull tried to enter a tent in their camp. Seaman's barking turned him away and made him leave the tent alone.

He watched for bears and barked continuously when any came near the camp. One evening Seaman discovered a bear eating the buffalo hides hanging on a pole at the edge of the camp. He al - erted Lewis in time to save the hides and keep everyone safe.

Seaman didn't always escape injury. He suffered a severed artery in his hind leg when a beaver bit him. Lewis and Clark performed emergency surgery to reconnect the artery and saved his life.

Lewis wrote that they saw many squirrels and he sent Seaman to catch them for food. A group of Indians wanted to purchase Seaman but Lewis refused their request.

In early 1806, Indians stole Seaman. The dog missed Captain Lewis and the rest of the group. Lewis threatened to send his men to kill the Indian tribe if they refused to return Seaman. The Indians agreed and Seaman rejoined the expedition. He was happy to see all of his friends again.

Once when one of the crew wounded a moose deer, Seaman worried that the injured deer would attack them. He followed it to the water, killed it, and brought it back to camp.

Mosquitoes attacked the men without mercy. Lewis wrote: "We can scarcely exist; for my own part I am confined by them to my bier (bed) at least ¾ of the time…my dog even howls with the tortures he experiences from them."

Seaman shared many special moments of history. He and Lewis explored the rivers, prairies, and mountains. They stood together smelling the air and gazing at the vastness of the Pacific Ocean. When the expedition returned to St. Louis, people met the party and celebrated. Throughout the celebrations, Seaman stayed by Lewis' side.

We do not know what happened to Seaman or how long he lived. I'm sure that as long as he lived, he protected Captain Lewis and his friends. Many books have been written about Seaman's role in the expedition.

He is honored in a number of expedition statues along the Lewis and Clark Trail from the beginning all the way to Oregon.

St. Charles, Missouri
Jefferson City, Missouri, State Capitol Grounds
Kansas City, Missouri, Case Park
Fort Calhoun, Nebraska, Fort Atkinson State Park
Sioux City, Iowa, Lewis and Clark Interpretive Center
Washburn, North Dakota, Lewis and Clark Interpretive Center
Great Falls, Montana, Overlook Mountain
Ft. Clatsop, Oregon, Ft. Clatsop National Memorial

Frontier Park, St. Charles, MO

Jefferson City, Missouri, State Capitol Grounds

The Captains' Return,
St. Louis, MO

Chapter 2

Balto, the Sled Dog

Siberian Huskies work as sled dogs in Alaska. When most of us would want to be curled up in front of a cozy fire, they work as a team pulling sleds in the bitter Alaskan cold — the deeper the snow and ice, the busier they are. Eight dogs pull the sled team — one of them is the leader. The sled driver is called a musher. This was the way people traveled in Alaska.

Balto was a sled dog in Alaska back in the 1920s. Cars and airplanes were still new and there weren't many ways for people to travel. In Nome, Alaska, one plane served the area only in the summertime.

In January of 1925, a diphtheria epidemic started in the town of Nome. Although diphtheria can be deadly for children, and spreads like fire, a vaccine had recently been discovered. When Dr. Curtis Welch treated several children who died of the disease, he sent a telegram to have a shipment of the vaccine serum mailed to him. He had ordered a supply in 1924 but it hadn't arrived.

A hospital in Anchorage had 300,000 units and sent their entire supply by train to Nenana. The only way to get the vaccine to Nome, 674 miles away, was by dog sled.

Balto and his team were at the last of the relay. With the serum loaded on their sled, they continued the long, hard journey through the driving wind and snow. The cold made it hard to breathe and the dogs panted for air. The blizzard nearly knocked over the sled and the team with its strong wind gusts. The dogs ran as fast and hard as they could while the musher fought to keep the sled from turning over. They stopped frequently to warm the serum. With forty degree below zero temperatures, it was nearly impossible to protect it from freezing. Nature put up a tough battle but the dogs fought on.

Many of the dogs died during the six days of hard travel. The mushers suffered severe frostbite. As reporters spread the word of the race against time, the world watched and cheered the teams onward.

Six days after the first team left Nenana, Balto led his team and his musher, Gunner Kaassen, into the streets of Nome. The serum arrived safely and in time to save the lives of the children in Nome. Balto became a famous hero, representing all the brave dogs that had worked so hard to save lives.

One year later, his admirers erected a statue in his honor in Central Park in New York City. The statue is still standing with a plaque that reads: Endurance — Fidelity — Intelligence.

Balto and some of his teammates traveled around the United States for a couple of years. He died in 1933. He has been the subject of a movie and several books.

Another lead dog, Togo, is not as well known but he led the longest and most difficult part of the relay. Togo was a black, brown, and gray Siberian Husky. His musher was Leonhard Seppala. Seppala tried to sell Togo several times when he was a puppy, but Togo always returned home.

One time Togo chased after Seppala's dog sled. Given the chance, it didn't take Togo long to prove that he was born to be a sled dog. He became the lead dog on the team for many years. He was twelve years old at the time of the diphtheria epidemic and the relay race by the sled dogs.

Togo led his team for two hundred and sixty miles, the longest stretch. During the last fifty-five miles, an eightymile an hour blizzard made it nearly impossible to run. Like Balto, Togo found it hard to see and to breathe but he fought to go on.

The annual Iditarod dog sled race was started in memory of this relay that became known as the "Great Race of Mercy."

Balto's run to Nome

Chapter 3

Hachiko, a loyal hero

Hachiko, a golden brown Akita, was born in Japan in 1923 and found his forever home with a man named Hidesaburo Ueno. Mr. Ueno was a professor at the University of Tokyo.

Hachiko loved his home. Professor Ueno rode the train into the city every morning and returned home in the evening after work. He had followed this schedule before he met Hachiko. The dog loved to walk with Mr. Ueno to the train every morning and returned every evening to wait for him to return.

They walked home and spent the rest of the night together. Hachiko never missed meeting the train and was always on time.

One day, Professor Ueno didn't come home. Hachiko waited and waited. Night time came and he still didn't come home. The professor had died suddenly during the day. Hachiko never knew what happened to him and refused to give up waiting. He returned to the station every evening to meet the train. Other people who rode the train every day began giving Hachiko food and treats.

For the rest of his life — the next nine years — Hachiko waited at the station every evening when the train was due.

In 1932, a newspaper article told the story of Hachiko waiting for Professor Ueno. Hachiko became famous throughout Japan. The people felt that he was an excellent example of family loyalty for children and adults.

A Japanese artist created a sculpture of Hachiko and people honored him for his faithfulness. Hachiko died in 1935. His monument is in Aoyama cemetery in Minatoku, Tokyo, next to Professor Ueno's grave.

Several statues honor Hachiko including one at the Tokyo train station. The exact spot where he waited each day is marked with bronze paw-prints. Hachiko has been the subject of books, video games, and movies.

Every year on April 8, a ceremony is held at the train station to remember him. Hundreds of Japanese citizens attend to honor his loyalty.

In 2009, Richard Gere starred in the movie, *Hachi: A Dog's Tale,* which told Hachiko's story.

CHAPTER 4

LAIKA, THE FIRST SPACE DOG

In 1957, Laika became the first living creature to travel in space and to orbit the earth. The Soviet Union launched the first satellite, Sputnik I on October 4. In November, they launched Sputnik 2 and Laika was aboard.

Laika had been a stray on the streets of Moscow. She was captured to become part of the space program. She was a friendly dog who liked everyone. She took part in all the preparation for the mission.

Laika on Sputnik I

Laika had a comfortable home on the space capsule. She did her part but she did not survive the trip. She had been placed in a special harness and provided with food and water. No one is sure when or why she died during the trip. The world learned later that there were never any plans to bring her home.

After Laika, another eleven dogs traveled in space before a man made the trip. Eight dogs returned alive and well. Four lost their lives.

A monument at Star City, near Moscow, honors the Russian cosmonauts who died during their missions. In one corner, a statue of a small dog with ears standing straight up, honors Laika. She earned her place in history.

The other space dogs were Bars, Lisichka, Belka, Strelka, Pchelka, Mushka, Damka, Krasavka, Chernushka, and Zvezdochka.

The final flight with dogs lasted twenty-two days in 1966. Verterok and Ugolyok were the dogs on that flight.

MASTER MCGRATH, A GREYHOUND FROM IRELAND

My mom wanted me to write about Master McGrath because our name is McGrath-Avery. Like Master McGrath, Mom's grandpa was born in County Waterford, Ireland.

Master McGrath was an Irish Greyhound born in 1866. He was one of seven puppies and was so small and weak they didn't know if he would live. No one thought he'd grow up to be a racing dog.

On his first race, he did so poorly that his trainer, James Galway, gave him away. Later when he started winning, Galway worked with him again. He grew up to break all records and win three Waterloo Cups (The Waterloo was a famous three-day Greyhound race in Liverpool, England).

He became the most famous dog in the world at that time. Queen Victoria and the Royal Family (of England) invited him and his owner, Lord Lurgan, to Windsor Castle. A song written about him became popular.

Master McGrath died in 1873 of heart disease but is still remembered at the Waterloo Cup events.

The last verse of Master McGrath's song:

"I've known many greyhounds that filled me with pride,

In the days that are gone, but it can't be denied,

that the greatest and the bravest that the world ever saw,

Was our champion of champions, great Master McGrath."

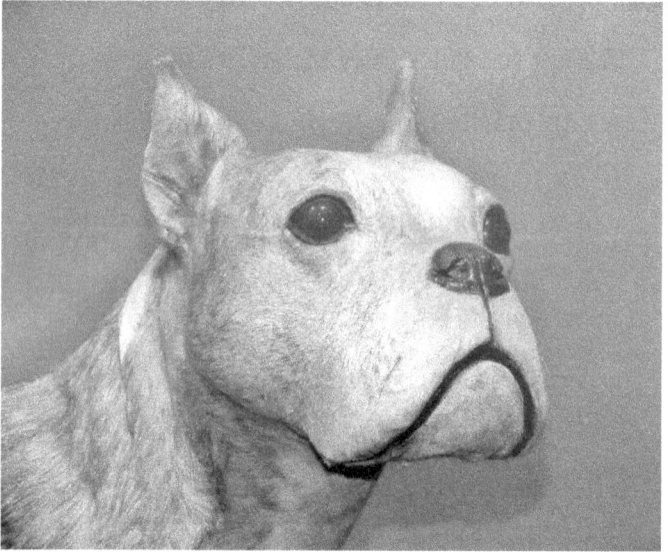

CHAPTER 6

SGT. STUBBY, THE FIRST AMERICAN WAR DOG

S tubby fought in World War I, which took place in the early part of the 20th century (from 1914 - 1918). He has been called the "George Washington of American war dogs."

No one knew where he came from or what kind of dog he was but he became famous. One day he wandered into a field where some soldiers were training in Connecticut. Corporal Robert Conroy, one of the soldiers, liked him. When Conroy shipped out, he hid Stubby on board. That's how Stubby became a soldier dog.

Stubby served on the front lines for eighteen long months. He took part in seventeen battles in Europe. He helped find and comfort wounded soldiers. He became famous when he saved his regiment from a surprise mustard gas (a deadly gas) attack. One time he actually caught and held a German spy by the seat of his pants until his unit caught up with him.

He served as a sergeant with the 102nd Infantry, 26th Yankee Division in France beginning on February 5, 1918. They remained under 24-hour a day fire for more than a month. He was wounded but recovered to continue his service. Stubby frequently left the trenches to look for wounded soldiers.

Poison gas nearly killed him and he became an expert at warning his unit of these attacks. With his superior ears, he warned the men of incoming artillery shells.

When Corporal Conroy was hospitalized with wounds, Stubby went with him and made friends with the staff and fellow patients. After their release, they rejoined their unit for the rest of the war.

When his unit saved a town, the women made Stubby a coat for his medals.

The soldiers loved and depended on him. When the war ended, General Pershing presented him with a gold medal and called him a "hero of the highest caliber." He visited both President Woodrow Wilson and President Calvin Coolidge in the White House.

He became a celebrity and continued to receive honors until his death in 1926. He became a lifetime member of the Red Cross, the American Legion

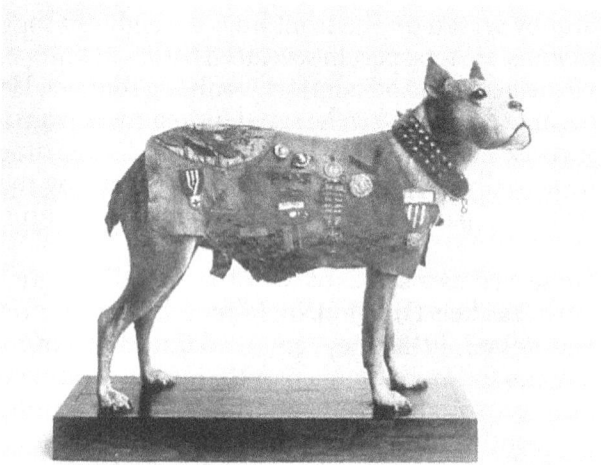

and the YMCA. The rest of his life, he marched in Legion parades and attended their conventions. The YMCA offered him three bones a day and a place to sleep for the rest of his life. He often traveled to promote Victory Bonds (sold to raise money for the war effort) and to recruit people to the Red Cross. Newspapers across the country published articles about Stubby.

Because of Stubby's success as a war dog, the U.S. Marines trained dogs that served in World War II.

When Corporal Conroy entered the Georgetown Law School, Stubby went with him. He became the Georgetown Hoyas' team mascot. At half-time, he entertained the fans by pushing the football around the field.

Stubby is featured at the Smithsonian in *The Price of Freedom: American at War* exhibit. In 2006, the World War I Memorial in Kansas City, Missouri, honored Stubby with a brick in the Walk of Honor.

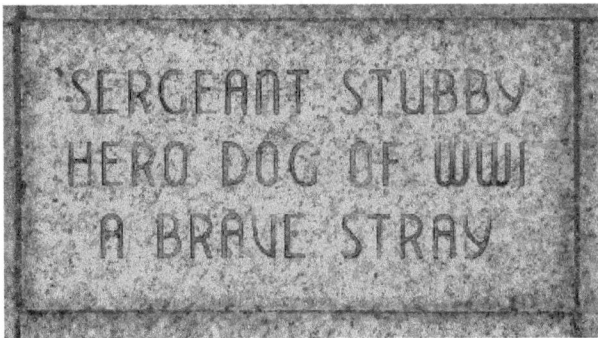

CHAPTER 7

WAR DOGS AND THE WAR DOG MEMORIAL

Y ou read about Stubby, the first American war dog, in the last chapter. Because of him, dogs took a bigger part in World War II and all wars since then.

Most war dogs are Doberman Pinschers, German Shepherds, Labrador Retrievers, or Collies that served with the U.S. Marine Corps.

In Guam, a U.S. territory, a memorial stands to honor all the dogs who lost their lives in World War II.

In 1935, the U.S. Marine Corps began training dogs to be scouts, couriers, and infantry dogs. They set up a school at Camp LeJeune, North Carolina. The dogs started with the rank of private — and just like the soldiers, they could get promoted. The dogs served with the Marines in the Pacific (in countries like Guam, Okinawa, Guadalcanal, and Iwo Jima).

Training school was long and hard. Dogs had basic training for six weeks. After that, they learned a specific job such as a messenger or scout dog. They were taught not to bark (what a hard lesson). Scout dogs learned to detect mines and enemy troops. They and their handlers were always first. Messenger dogs carried things — notes and supplies. The infantry dogs used their noses to let soldiers know if the Japanese were nearby. They saved the lives of many of our soldiers.

The memorial in Guam includes a life-sized statue of a Doberman pinscher laying on a plaque that names the dogs that sacrificed their lives in the battle for Guam.

There is a replica of the memorial at the University of Tennessee College of Veterinary Science in Knoxville.

CHAPTER 8

SGT. REX

Sgt. Rex is a German Shepherd who became famous for his work as a Marine dog. German Shepherds have a great sense of smell. He served three tours in Iraq during his military career as a bomb-sniffing dog.

Trained by the Air Force as part of the Military Working Dog Program, he served in the U.S. Marine Corps.

A dog is trained for a specific job. Sgt. Rex learned the smells of many different explosive materials. His job was to find bombs and warn his partner and the other Marines in his unit. He served his first tour of duty with Mike Dowling, who later wrote a book about their experiences. The name of the book is Sergeant Rex: The Unbreakable Bond Between a Marine and His Military Working Dog.

He served two more tours of duty with a new partner, Corporal Megan Leavey. He and Corporal Leavey became good friends and depended on each other. In 2006, a bomb exploded near them and both Sgt. Rex and Corporal Leavey were badly hurt. Corporal Leavey was sent back to New York and later retired.

Sgt. Rex stayed in the Marines and after he recovered, he worked at Camp Pendleton. He never went back to Iraq. He and Corporal Leavey missed each other.

In 2012, the Marine Corps decided to retire him because he suffered from a facial paralysis that kept him from his bomb-sniffing duties. When Corporal Leavey found out, she wanted to adopt him and take him home. She gained the support of many people and with their help, the Marine Corps agreed to return him to her.

Now the two veterans continue to love and take care of each other.

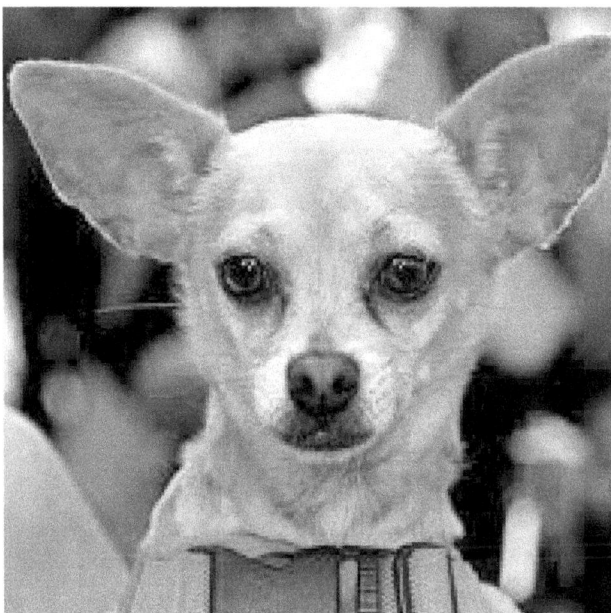

CHAPTER 9

GIDGET, THE TACO BELL CHIHUAHUA

Everyone knew and loved the Taco Bell dog. Gidget, a Chihuahua, was born in 1994. When she was eight weeks old, she met Sue Chipperton, a dog trainer. Sue began training her and for the rest of Gidget's life, they worked together. She became a star when Taco Bell hired her as their mascot. Although she was a girl, she played a boy dog whose famous line was "Yo Quiero Taco Bell."

After her commercials aired, Taco Bell sold more food. People loved her. Gidget charmed everyone she

met and traveled first-class everywhere she went. She even opened up the New York Stock Exchange and made an appearance at Madison Square Garden in New York City.

She loved the pampering and attention. That always made people want to pamper her even more.

She appeared in two movies and did commercials for an insurance company. When she retired from acting, she loved going on hikes and beach visits. She liked to sleep in the sun and enjoyed her many fans.

In 2009, Gidget had a stroke and died in Los Angeles, California.

CHAPTER 10

BUD JACKSON, FIRST CROSS COUNTRY TRAVELER

Horatio Nelson Jackson, a doctor from Vermont, loved the new invention, the automobile. Even though he didn't own a car, he believed that everyone would soon use them for travel. In 1903, while he visited San Francisco, he agreed to a $50 bet that he could drive an automobile across the country. He had taken driving lessons but he didn't own a car.

Dr. Jackson convinced a mechanic, Sewall Crocker, to make the trip with him. He bought a used 20-

hp car, named it the Vermont, and filled it with the supplies he purchased. He carried extra coats, sleeping bags, blankets, canteens and other supplies he thought they might need.

Jackson and Crocker left San Francisco on May 23. He soon blew a tire and had to replace the side lanterns (used instead of the headlights we now have). The car broke down and trouble seemed to follow them until the reached Idaho.

In many places, roads had not yet been built. They drove across pastures, fields and along paths. The rough ride caused parts to shake loose. It's hard today to imagine the noisy pioneer car, the rough paths they drove across, the long drives between towns and restaurants, the lack of communication

In Caldwell, Dr. Jackson bought a dog, a pit bull named Bud. The doctor had wanted a dog so finding Bud gave him hope for a successful trip.

Bud loved riding in the car but he developed a problem. The car had no windshield or roof and the dust caused his eyes to hurt and water. Dr. Jackson saw the problem and found a pair of goggles that would fit Bud. He later got sick from drinking bad water, but he loved riding in the car

As they passed through towns, people cheered them. Reporters took their pictures and interviewed them. People loved seeing the automobile with three passengers — Dr. Jackson, Crocker and Bud in his goggles.

The car continued to break down but they would stop, order more parts and wait until they arrived. Somewhere in Idaho, Dr. Jackson lost his coat that contained most of his money. They got lost in Wyoming and went without food for a day and a half before a sheepherder saw them and offered them food. Bud woke up every day ready to jump in the car and ride some more.

By July 12, they reached Omaha, Nebraska, roughly half way across the country. As they drove east, the roads improved and they had fewer problems. However, when they reached Buffalo, New York, the car hit something in the road and all three of them were thrown from the car. Luckily, no one was hurt. They climbed back in the car and drove on.

On July 26, sixty-three and a half days and 5600 miles after they left San Francisco, they drove into New York City, the first to drive across the country. They had used more than 800 gallons of gas.

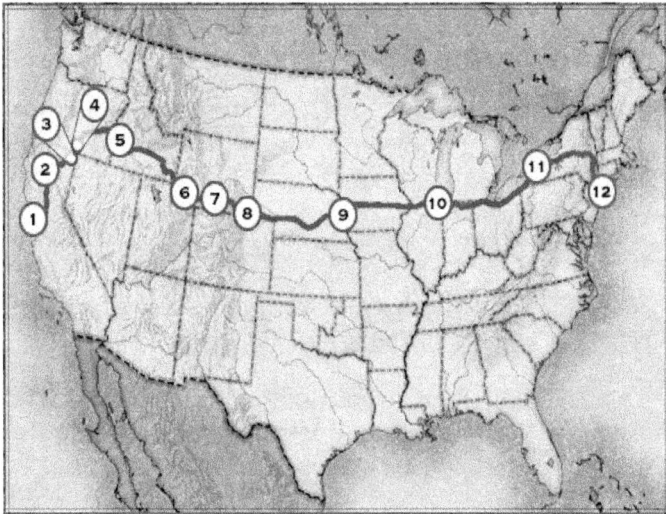

Bud's Route Across the USA

Bud became famous as the first dog to make this long journey. Dr. Jackson returned to his home in Burlington, Vermont. It didn't take long for Bud to become a valued family member. He and Dr. Jackson often rode around town together. He died in 1913, at the age of ten. He is buried on the Jackson grounds that he loved to roam. His goggles and pictures are on display at the Smithsonian in Washington, DC.

Bud's Display at the Smithsonian

CHAPTER 11

BOBBIE, THE WONDER DOG

Bobbie was a Scotch Collie/English Shepherd dog born in Oregon in 1921. He lived with his family, Mr. and Mrs. Frank Brazier, in Silverton in the area known as the Willamette Valley. When he was two years old, the family took a trip to Indiana, more than 2,000 miles away from home.

While they were in Indiana, Bobbie lost his family. He learned later that they searched everywhere for him before they had to return home. They missed him as much as he missed them. The Braziers thought they would never see Bobbie again.

However, Bobbie loved his family and knew he would do whatever it took to find them again. He set out to find his way back to Oregon. He traveled in good weather and bad, across the plains, the desert and the mountains to reach his home. His nose and his sense of direction led him. Hunger, thirst and all the dangers of travel couldn't stop him. He was alone and lonely. It took nearly seven months.

Bobby's Grave

It's hard to imagine how badly he wanted to find his family. When he finally reached home, his paws were worn all the way to the bone. Bobbie had lost a lot of weight and looked mangy. His family immediately knew that he had walked all the way.

Mr. and Mrs. Brazier could hardly believe he had found his way back into their lives. Their family was complete again.

Reporters learned of his unbelievable journey home and Bobbie was soon famous. He received letters from around the world. Articles and books were written about him. *Ripley's Believe It or Not* featured his story. He even played in a movie, *The Call of the West*.

His loyalty to his family amazed people. Silverton's annual children's pet parade still honors him each year. There is a mural on a wall in downtown Silverton. He received medals and keys to cities.

When he died in 1927, he was buried with honors in Portland, Oregon. Rin Tin Tin, the movie star dog, laid a wreath at his grave. A red-and-white dog house sits next to his grave.

CHAPTER 12

DEWEY, THE LIBRARY CAT

Vicki Myron was the librarian at the public library in a small Iowa town called Spencer.

One cold January morning in 1988, when she opened up the library, she found a kitten in the book return box. She took him inside and showed him to the rest of the staff. They immediately decided they wanted to adopt him.

The library board and city council agreed and the kitten had a home. They named him Dewey

Readmore Books and he became a member of the staff.

People from near and far donated money to help care for Dewey. Visitors showed up just to see him. He became the main greeter to the library patrons.

"Country Magazine" and "Cat Fancy Magazine" wrote feature articles about Dewey. Television and radio stations talked about him. He was featured in books and starred in "Puss in Books," a video documentary about library cats.

The library staff gave Dewey his own job description. It included such duties as "reducing stress for all humans pay attention to him," "sitting by the front door at 9 am every morning to greet people," and "climbing in book bags and briefcases."

Dewey did his job well.

The staff found him a very finicky eater and finding food he liked was a challenge.

Dewey died in 2006 from a stomach tumor at the age of nineteen. People still miss his morning greeting.

Dewey became a hero in his hometown and will always be remembered. Vicki Myron has written several books about Dewey the library cat.

Dewey, The Library Cat

Chapter 13

Higgins, the Movie Star

Most people know Higgins by one of his most famous characters, "Benji."

Born in 1957, he started life as a mutt (probably part Miniature Poodle, Schnauzer, and Cocker Spaniel). When he was a puppy, Frank Inn, an animal trainer, rescued him from the Burbank Animal Shelter in California.

Higgins grew up to be a movie star. He played in 1960s television shows including "Petticoat

Junction," "Green Acres," and "The Beverly Hill-billies." He won a Patsy Award in 1967 (an award for animals performing in television shows). He played the character, Dog, in "Petticoat Junction" for six seasons.

He was a good actor with great expressions. Frank Inn said Higgins was the smartest dog he'd ever trained. They worked together for years and Mr. Inn took pride in teaching Higgins a new routine for every television episode.

Fans loved Higgins. He won their hearts with his ability to express emotion. He knew many special tricks and easily performed them. On cue, he would

Benji

sneeze, yawn, climb a ladder, or open the mailbox and take out a letter.

The key to the success of Higgins and his trainer was teamwork. Higgins proved to be the most expressive dog in the history of film. Frank's training was so good that Higgins took his cues from whomever he worked with on the set.

Higgins and Edgar Buchanan (Uncle Joe on "Petticoat Junction") became good friends. They worked together in the series and in "Benji." It became the last movie for both of them.

Higgins retired when he was eleven but, at the age of 14, he came out of retirement and played the title role in "Benji." It became the biggest role in his career and became the third largest-grossing film of the year. Benji died in 1975 at the age of 17. In later "Benji" shows, his daughter, Benjean, played the title role.

"Benji" brought attention to mixed breed shelter dogs. The American Humane Society credits the movie with promoting over a million shelter adoptions nationwide.

CHAPTER **14**

DAKOTA, THE **101**ST SENATOR

Dakota is a Bichon with a special and important job. He helps our senators make laws for our country. He is so popular on Capitol Hill (the place where the senators work) that he has been named the 101st Senator (there are 100 senators — two from each of the fifty states).

Senator Kent Conrad is Dakota's human companion. He was elected by the people of North Dakota to serve in the United States Senate in Washington, DC.

Dakota is Senator Conrad's assistant at work. He follows the senator up and down the hallways of the Capitol, attends meetings, and improves the morale of everyone he works with.

It is not uncommon for the congressional leaders to bring their dogs to work with them. Since politics is often stressful, the dogs provide a sense of calm that is usually helpful. Since the beginning of our country, dogs have been a part of the congressional process.

Senator Conrad rescued Dakota from a shelter after he had been found abandoned and starving. Dakota immediately became part of his forever family but he still remembers being left alone. Because he gets upset when everyone leaves, the senator decided to take him to work every day.

In the following picture, Dakota accompanies Senator Conrad to a meeting.

Dakota loves his job. He gets plenty of exercise running back and forth from one meeting to another. He enjoys seeing the other senators and all the people who work in the Capitol. Sometimes, he prefers to stay in Senator Conrad's office and take a nap while everyone else works.

Dakota isn't the only dog that helps run our country. Several senators depend on their dogs to keep people happy.

Since Dakota was rescued from near starvation, he has suffered medical problems. He is currently battling cancer.

Chapter 15

Smoky, a Decorated War Heroine

Smoky was a four-pound Yorkshire Terrier (Yorkie) who lived during World War II. She was found in an abandoned foxhole in New Guinea in 1944. The war was up close to the people in the countries and islands in the Pacific Ocean.

Bill Wynne, an American soldier adopted her and the two became good friends. Bill's buddies fell in love with the little dog and she became the mascot for the 5th Air Force's 26th Recon Squadron.

She won a mascot contest from "Yank Down Under" magazine.

Corporal Wynne was on a ship during the Luzon Invasion (Luzon is in the Philippines). It was attacked by a Japanese plane and ran aground. Corporal Wynne grabbed Smoky, tucked her under his arm and waded to shore.

When the soldiers arrived on land, they needed to set up communications. To do this they needed to string telephone wire under an airport runway. An eight-inch drainage pipe under the airstrip was clogged with dirt and sand. None of the men could crawl through it. Corporal Wynne was asked if Smoky could crawl through with the wire attached to her collar.

Corporal Wynne put Smoky at one end of the pipe with his buddies. He ran to the other end and called Smoky. She was afraid but when he continued to call her, she trusted him and started through the pipe. Corporal Wynne continued to call her, "Come, Smoky... ."

One of Smoky's Memorials

She slowly crawled through the pipe and even in the dark, her eyes searched for Corporal Wynne's face. She knew she had to be brave. As she moved closer to him, she crawled faster. Soon she started running. When she reached the end of the pipe, she ran straight into Corporal Wynne's arms. All the soldiers cheered. An officer treated Smoky to her own steak dinner that night.

Smoky remained with the squadron for the rest of the war. However, when it was time for the soldiers to return home to the United States, Smoky would not be permitted to board the ship because of Army rules.

Corporal Wynne decided to smuggle Smoky aboard. He put her in an oxygen-mask case and walked on board with her.

She lived with Corporal Wynne the rest of her life. She died in 1957 and is buried in a park in Cleveland, Ohio. There are six memorials in her honor and she is recognized as the first therapy dog because she visited so many soldiers in military hospitals.

Smokey was credited with twelve combat missions and awarded eight battle stars.

Chapter 16

Owney, the United States Post Office Mascot

Owney was a mixed Terrier who was abandoned as a puppy in the late 1880s. A postal worker, Owen, found and adopted him. Owen worked at the Albany, New York, post office.

After wandering into the back door of the post office, Owney made his bed on a mail bag. Owen's co-workers liked the dog and gave him his name. He soon became the post office's mascot.

Owney slept on the mail bags. When the postal workers moved the bags, Owney rode along with them. When the mail was delivered to different post offices where the workers welcomed Owney. He protected the mail until a mail clerk took it.

Once when a mail pouch fell out of a delivery wagon, Owney stayed and guarded it. He curled up on the bag and didn't move until the mail clerks found him hours later.

He became the mascot for the United States Postal Service and traveled throughout the United States (over 140,000 miles) for nine years. In all that time, he was never in a train wreck.

On a trip to Montreal, Canada, the postmaster put him in a kennel and wouldn't release him until the Albany clerks paid a fee for dog food. When international mail service began, Owney made an around-the-world trip, riding by train or ship, however the mail was carried. The four-month trip took Owney to Asia, North Africa, the Middle East, and Europe.

As he traveled more, the Albany workers worried he'd get lost. They bought him a collar with a tag that said, "Owney, Post Office, Albany, New York." As he continued to travel, other post offices added their tags. The Postmaster General gave him a coat to put the tags on. Soon he had too many tags and too much weight to carry. At one time, it was reported that Owney had over a thousand tags.

He received medals too, for "Best Traveled Dog" and "Globe Trotter."

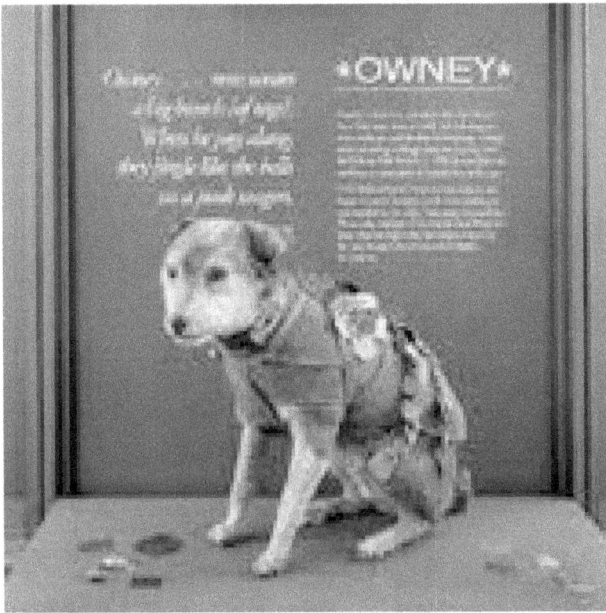

Owney died in 1897. Today the Smithsonian in Washington, DC, is home to an "Owney" exhibit. In 2011, the United States Postal Service issued a forever stamp in his honor.

CHAPTER 17

TRAKR, THE RESCUE DOG

Trakr was a German Shepherd born in the Czech Republic in 1994. He was trained as a police dog and assigned to a Canadian police officer in Halifax, Nova Scotia.

Officer James Symington became Trakr's handler in 1995 and the two worked together in Halifax for six years. Trakr helped in the arrests of many criminals and helped find missing people.

He was retired early and Symington took a medical leave.

When the planes hit the World Trade Center in New York City on September 11, 2001, Symington and Trakr watched the search and rescue operations on television. They drove 1,500 miles to New York and arrived early on September 12. That morning, Trakr found someone buried under the rubble. Firefighters dug out Genelle Guzman, who was the last of twenty survivors who had been inside the buildings when they collapsed.

Symington and Trakr

Two days later, Trakr passed out from breathing too many chemicals and too much smoke. After he recovered, he and Symington returned to Halifax.

They received an "Extraordinary Service to Humanity Award" for their help. Time magazine named Trakr one of history's most heroic animals. Newspapers, magazines, and television shows have featured his story.

Symington and Trakr moved to Los Angeles, California. As he grew older, Trakr lost the use of his back legs. He died in 2009.

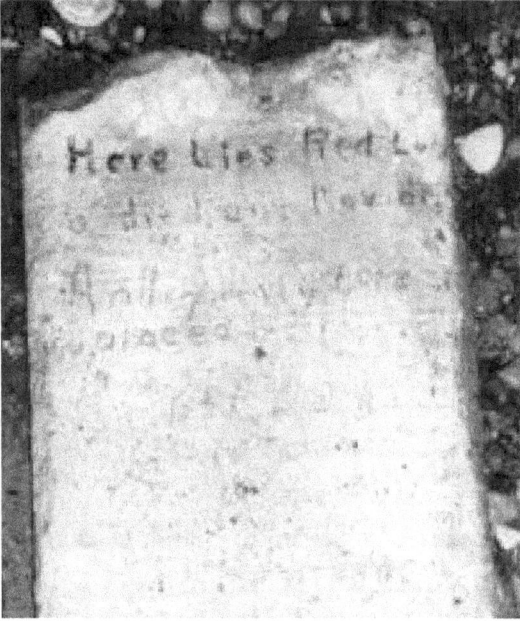

Here Lies Red L...

CHAPTER 18

RED LADY

The sailors liked the shy little yellow dog that they found. They played with her and never suspected that she would become so important to their lives as the Coast Guard Beach Patrol "Sand Pounders" who guarded the coast of Padre Island during World War II.

In 1941, after the Japanese attacked Pearl Harbor in Hawaii, the Americans joined the Allied Forces in World War II. Germany, Italy, and Japan became our enemies.

German submarines roamed the Gulf of Mexico and damaged more than 160 U.S. ships. Dead bodies washed ashore on Padre Island and people in Port Isabel heard loud explosions out in the Gulf.

Americans feared that Nazi Germany would land spies on shore through the Texas coast. The Sand Pounders patrolled the island with specially trained dogs. The sailors liked their canine team but these dogs were their partners and would never be playmates.

One day when the sailors visited the mainland to pick up supplies, they found the little dog and started playing fetch with her. The dog chased the stick and brought it back to them. They played for close to an hour and threw about 200 sticks before it was time to go back to the island. The dog fell in love with her newfound friends.

When it was time to leave, the sailors left her behind, jumped in their jeep and drove to the ferry that would take them across the bay. However, she wasn't about to lose these new friends she'd found. She followed them and jumped in the jeep just as it was ready to board the ferry. None of the sailors said a word about her until they were too far out in the bay to return her. Her tail wagged her joy and excitement.

The young sailors were as happy as she was. Most of them had left dogs at home when they left to serve their country. They needed a dog friend as much as the dog needed people friends.

She'd been alone for so long she didn't remember ever having a name. It was good to have a home and she wagged her thanks every time they sailors suggested a name. They never agreed so she remained without a name until Captain Johansen returned to the island. His men had given him the nickname, Old Red-Lead Joe, because he made them paint every piece of equipment with red lead to protect it from the sand and water.

One day while the sailors painted equipment, one of them brushed red lead on the dog's coat. The captain saw her and said, "I see you've red-leaded the little lady." The men liked his response and named the dog, Red Lady.

Every day Red Lady played with the sailors. She loved playing ball and sneaking a snack out of the back door of the mess hall. Her favorite activity was racing alongside, and then jumping aboard, the jeeps when they went out on patrol. The sailors loved to catch her when she jumped in.

They added joy to each other's lives and she was happy to be their mascot.

One day as Red Lady raced along a jeep, she stumbled and fell under the wheels. The jeep couldn't stop in time to keep from crushing the dog. The heartbroken men couldn't believe they'd lost their friend. They buried her on the top of a tall sand dune and engraved a headstone for her.

"Here lies Red Lady who died one November day
and gently here is placed to stay.
She left everyone (of 81 men) with an aching heart,
because with that timid dog we could not part.
Our dear little mascot who was so shy
deserves a salute from everyone passing by."

All the men on the island mourned her death and attended her funeral.

As the war drew to a close and the men went home, they took their memories of Red Lady with them. Years later in 1963, Ila Loetscher, who would be known as "The Turtle Lady," found Red Lady's gravestone while she was driving the beach searching for sea turtle nests. She wanted to know more about the dog.

Four years later Ed Syers, a journalist, wrote about Ila's search for information about the dog. Lon Seebach, one of the Sand Pounders who served on the island, read Ed's article. He contacted Ila and told her how much the men had loved Red Lady.

Many years later, Steve Hathcock, South Padre Island's historian, wrote the whole story and brought Red Lady back to her place in the island's history.

The photograph below shows a World War II working dog on the South Padre Island beach patrol.

CHAPTER 19

GABE, IRAQI VETERAN AND WAR HERO

Every year the American Humane Society presents a "Hero Dog of the Year Award." The award celebrates the devotion between dogs and people.

Gabe, a ten-year-old Labrador Retriever mix, won the 2012 award. Sgt. First Class Gabe, United States Army, completed more than 200 combat missions in Iraq before his retirement. Working with his handler, Sgt. First Class Chuck Shuck, he was the most successful detection dog in Iraq for 2006 and 2007.

Gabe is a rescue dog. He lived in a Houston, Texas animal shelter. One day before he was to be euthanized, he was adopted and taken to Lackland Air Force Base to be trained as a military dog. There, he met Shuck.

After his training, he and Shuck shipped to Iraq in 2006. Gabe's job was to detect bombs. With his superior nose, he sniffed out explosives and materials. His intelligence and dedication enabled him to find the enemy's guns and ammunition. By doing his job, he helped save the lives of many soldiers.

In addition to Iraq, Gabe has been stationed at Fort Lewis, Washington; Ft. Bliss, Texas; Ft. Leonard Wood, Missouri; and Ft. Hood, Texas.

Gabe, who has more than 33,000 Facebook friends, wrote:

> *"I started my duty in 2006 when I deployed to Iraq. I was fortunate enough to work with some truly amazing soldiers. My job was to find hidden guns and explosives and to help keep our soldiers safe. While deployed, I completed over 210 combat missions with 26 finds of explosives and weapons. I also visited wounded troops in combat hospitals and visited children in elementary schools."*

While they were in Iraq another dog-handler team lost their lives, Cpl. Kory Weins and Cooper died in a roadside bomb attack. It's a dangerous job even for the experts in sniffing out bombs.

Gabe the Hero

Gabe and Shuck survived when a roadside bomb hit the jeep they were riding in. Another time they survived a shootout in an Iraqi village.

Gabe frequently visited the wounded troops in military hospitals. He enjoyed representing the

U.S. Army whenever needed. While on duty, Gabe earned more than 40 awards including three Army Commendation medals and an Army Achievement medal.

Stationed with field artillery units, Gabe eventually became sensitive to the loud booms of the guns. Today he is frightened by thunder and other loud noises.

Gabe retired from the U.S. Army in 2009, and Shuck adopted him. The two now spend their time trying to bring awareness to folks about the plight of shelter dogs, and the importance of adopting these very special canines into a forever home. Gabe enjoys meeting people and especially likes to visit schools.

By winning the 2012 Hero Dog Award, Gabe won $15,000 for his favorite charity, the U.S. War Dogs Association, which provides care packages for deployed soldiers, marines, airmen, and their K-9 partners.

Gabe also won the 2008 American Kennel Club's Heroic Military Working Dog Award

CHAPTER 20

TIFFANY, THERAPY DOG AND AWARD-WINNING AGILITY COMPETITOR

S mall dogs have big hearts and Tiffany, a 14-year-old Yorkshire Terrier, is living proof of a dog who brings joy to others. She has earned her "award-winning dog" status in several areas. Tiffany has made more than 700 visits to nursing homes, earning her the Therapy Dog International 500 Gold Award (TDIG).

Tiffany and her human friend, Phyllis Bandi, enrolled in dog obedience class and at the end of the first year, Tiffany earned her CGC (Canine Good Citizen) and

TDI (Therapy Dog International). They then started visiting nursing homes and children in daycare centers.

When she visits nursing homes, Tiffany brings smiles and joy as she entertains the seniors with her agility displays. Afterwards, she's always ready for the love and attention that her audience gives her. Many seniors experience loneliness and need exercise motivation. Petting a dog requires a physical interaction and fosters movement in stiffened joints. Like other therapy dogs, Tiffany offers love and acceptance. She often reminds people of the dog companions of their earlier years. She provides plenty of opportunities for smiles and laughter. The effects of her visit last long after she has gone home.

Day after day, week in and week out, the years passed and Tiffany, like the people she visited, became a senior. During all of her time walking the hallways, sitting with the residents as well as entertaining all who were interested, Tiffany became a true champion in the minds and hearts of all who had the opportunity to meet her.

She loves agility for fun and exercise. She knows how to stay young. She holds her Tach 3 award (Teacup Agility Champion). Agility requires lots of training. Tiffany's intelligence and love of exercise made her a natural for doggie sports competitions. In February 2012, the Wall Street Journal featured Tiffany on their front page, showcasing her agility skills and talent.

Tiffany with her many ribbons and awards

Tiffany loves getting groomed and having her picture taken with her many ribbons.

Tiffany has played Toto in the Wizard of Oz and Chowsie in Gypsy. She enjoys her "star" roles and appreciates all of the attention. However, visiting her senior friends has always been her favorite activity.

She lives in Pittsburgh, Pennsylvania, with her mom and dad. She has a little sister, Amber, who is also an award-winning Yorkshire Terrier.

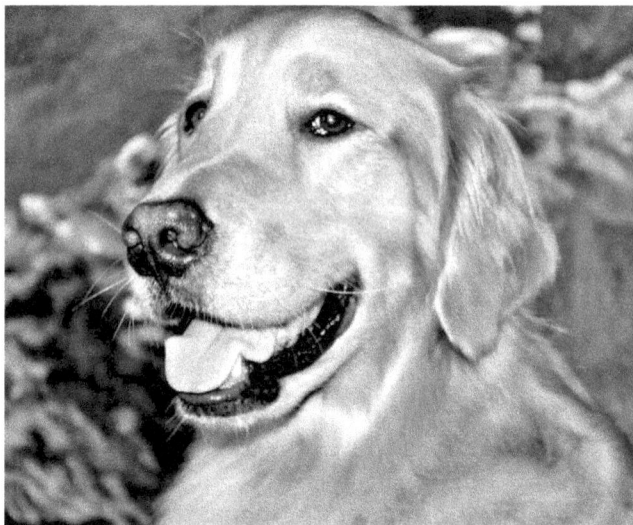

CHAPTER 21

TUESDAY, PSYCHIATRIC THERAPY DOG

Tuesday's training started when he was just three days old. While his eyes were still closed, his legs wouldn't carry him, and his only awareness was touch, his trainers started to develop his interaction with humans. Born and raised to be a therapy dog, his trainers needed to teach this baby Golden Retriever to interact with humans. Tuesday was born and bred to become an assistant to a disabled person.

Tuesday with Luis

To keep him from bonding with one person, many different trainers worked with him. When he was six months old, he was taken to a prison to continue with a special prisoner dog-training program. He learned much but his heart broke when his trainer was paroled.

He was two years old before he found his forever assignment with Luis Montalvan, a disabled Iraqi veteran. Luis suffered from physical and psychological war injuries. He desperately needed a therapy dog.

After serving two tours in Iraq, Luis suffered from PTSD, nightmares, a traumatic brain injury, panic attacks, severe headaches, and fractured vertebrae. He retreated from the world, his family included. He seldom left his apartment and turned down a good job because he knew he couldn't handle it. He needed a therapy dog.

He found Tuesday in 2008, and his psychological wounds began to mend. Tuesday takes care of Luis and provides him with constant companionship, love, and attention. He knows when Luis's heart starts beating faster, when he becomes fearful or anxious, when he needs help, and when he simply needs attention.

Tuesday and Luis at beach

Tuesday spends every minute of every day with Luis. They play together, go places together, and work together. When Luis worked on his book, *Until Tuesday*, the dog stayed with him each step of the way. He attends book signings and presentations with him. They are a team. If you get Luis, you get Tuesday, and vice versa.

Tuesday spent the first two years of his life preparing to bond with one person and to support his needs. He walks beside Luis, reminds him when it's time to take his pills, soothes his emotional stress, helps him keep his balance when he has vertigo attacks, pick up something for him when he drops it ,and gives him constant love.

When Luis received his master's degree from Columbia University's School of Journalism in 2010, Tuesday wore a cap and gown and received his own diploma.

Tuesday is living the life his trainers wished for him and because of that, Luis Montalvan is living a life he thought he had lost forever. Together they travel around the country explaining how service dogs can help our wounded soldiers.

You can learn more about Luis and Tuesday in the book, *Until Tuesday,* or at www.luismontalvan.net.

Chapter 22
Sauer, the world's greatest
tracker

Sauer, a Doberman Pinscher, was born at the South African Police Dogs School near Capetown, South Africa in 1917.

As a puppy, he showed little potential for police work. Detective Sergeant Herbert Kruger became his trainer and Sauer developed a strong relationship with him. Kruger, a patient handler, taught Sauer well.

In a demonstration that garnered attention, Sauer followed a trail that was 132 hours old. He was soon in demand to track thieves. Once when a minister was preaching at his church, a thief broke into his home and stole cash and a bag of clothes. More than a day later, Sauer was taken to the place where the thief had dumped the bag. He picked up the trail, which led him to a house. Sauer started barking at the door. When it was opened, he ran straight to the thief.

He continued to show extraordinary tracking powers. In Paaupan, a thief left his knife at the scene of the crime. Sauer tracked him for several miles along a railway line. He successfully followed him to a shop where the thief left a bag and followed him eight miles into the veld (a wide open rural area). Sauer tracked him a total of 26 miles before catching him in a railway station.

Sergeant Kruger and Sauer continued to work together whenever someone requested their help.

In 1925 by scent only, Sauer tracked a thief for 100 miles across the Great Karoo (a desert region in South Africa) without stopping. He set a tracking record that has never been broken.

Sauer died in 1926 when he was nine. The police buried him in a place of honor on their property.

CHAPTER 23

SEAMUS AND LILY,
CONSERVATION DOGS

Dogs play a valuable role in conservation. Trainers select them for their ability and willingness to work. They train the dogs in the same methods as police and search-and-rescue dogs. All dogs must have high energy levels and the ability to focus. They are trained to search for specific obnoxious weeds, animal locations, pharmaceuticals, and heavy metals.

Working Dogs for Conservation (WDC) sends teams of dogs to international locations including tropical forests in Asia and Africa, the Arctic, national parks, wildlife refuges, and more. Only one in 1,000 dogs meet their high work standards.

WDC assigns each dog to a handler who trains the dog and handles it in the field. They live and work together because they must totally understand each other and become a team. Like a person, a good dog will be able to adjust to necessary changes in the field.

Seamus, a Border Collie adopted from the Heart of the Valley Animal Shelter in Bozeman, Montana, is the youngest in a pack of dogs at Working Dogs for Conservation.

Seamus

His expertise is searching for an invasive weed called Dyer's Woad on Mount Sentinel in Montana and kit fox scat in California.

Lily

Lily, a Yellow Lab/Southern Belle Cross, is another working dog. She was adopted from Smartcritters in Lawrenceville, Georgia.

Highly intelligent, her specialty is looking for invasive Chinese bush clover and emerald ash borer, and the scat of grizzly and black bears, and the Cross River gorilla in Cameroon.

The gorilla is an example of the projects these dogs encounter. The Cross River Gorillas are the most endangered great apes in the world. They avoid people and live their lives in secrecy. Working Dogs for Conservation joined with the Wildlife Conservation Society, the North Carolina Zoo and the Smithsonian Institute to help locate, study, and protect them.

CHAPTER 24

DRAKE AND DEKE, THE DUCKS
UNLIMITED MASCOTS

D rake spent years as the Ducks Unlimited mascot. Raised and trained by Mike Stewart of Wildrose Kennels, Drake is skilled in retrieving ducks during a hunt.

Drake is a 72-pound Black Labrador Retriever. As a star on Ducks Unlimited TV, Drake enjoyed lots of attention and the opportunity to showcase his extraordinary skill. He starred in a series of training videos, which became the longest running program of its type to air on television.

Sporting dogs live an outdoor lifestyle, always training and hunting in the field. Drake's life has been filled with both and he enjoyed them equally. Drake hunted throughout the US and Canada, and made public appearances at DU festivals, banquets, and fundraising events. In 2004, he served on the first US Gundog Team to ever compete in the United Kingdom. The team won the P&O Irish Sea International Championship.

Mike Stewart wrote of a hunt in Alaska: "The longest retrieve I ever made with Drake was in the flats, estimated between 500 and 600 yards out

across the mud flats, a total blind. By the time he reached the bird, he was completely out of sight…"

Drake is now retired and his role as mascot has passed to Deke, a younger Black Lab who spends his days in training, filming and hunting.

Chapter 25

Old Drum

During his life, Old Drum was an ordinary hound dog. He lived with his owner, Charles Burden. Old Drum lived a simple life and he became famous only after his death. Dog lovers everywhere would soon learn about him. Because of him, dogs would forever be known as "man's best friend."

Some dogs in the countryside had been killing sheep and Leonidas Hornsby, Charles' brother-in-law, swore to kill the next dog he saw on his property. Unfortunately Old Drum happened to be the one.

On October 18, 1869, Leonidas told his nephew to shoot the dog. When Charles found Old Drum's body, he was so angry about the loss of his friend that he sued Leonidas. The case went through several trials before the final and most famous one in Warrensburg, Missouri. Charles hired a lawyer, George Graham Vest, who in his closing argument to the jury made one of the best-ever tributes to a dog. In it he stated:

> *"The one absolutely unselfish friend that man can have in this selfish world, the one that never deserts him and the one that never proves ungrateful or treacherous is his dog."*

Although that speech won the case, Leonidas eventually took it all the way to the Missouri Supreme Court. Charles won again.

Old Drum is buried in Cass County, Missouri (south of Kansas City) but his memorial is located in Warrensburg on the Johnson County Courthouse lawn.

George Graham Vest had served in the Confederate Congress during the Civil War and later served in the Missouri Congress and the U.S. Senate. However, he remains most famous for his "man's best friend" eulogy to Old Drum.

To read the entire speech, visit:

http://www.historyplace.com/speeches/vest.htm.

Old Drum Memorial

LUKE'S CONCLUSION

There you have it — dogs and a cat that have changed, and are changing, history every day. Like the people they shared their experiences with, they did their best to make their world a better place.

I believe that the world is better because of them and that they offer dogs and people strong proof that each of us can make our world better. I love my family and love to tell stories about other dogs.

To my fellow dogs — the twenty-six dogs and one cat that I shared with you should really make each of us proud. I want to be like them. How about you?

To all the human readers — if you don't have a dog, or a cat, in your life, you are missing the companionship and support of a good friend. I hope you enjoyed reading about these awesome animals.

They are all heroes!

www.ingramcontent.com/pod-product-compliance
Lightning Source LLC
Chambersburg PA
CBHW071906020426
42331CB00010B/2695